IMPROVISE, GIRL, IMPROVISE

LILITH LATINI

Library of Congress Cataloging-in-Publication Data is available.

ISBN 978-1-62729-012-8 -- (paperback)

10 9 8 7 6 5 4 3 2 1

Cover design by Robyn Kanner

*For the friends who are my family
and my sweet parents from New Jersey*

How did I survive apocalyptic fire?
I simply refused to feel the flames.

EMMA FROST, *Dark Reign: The Cabal*

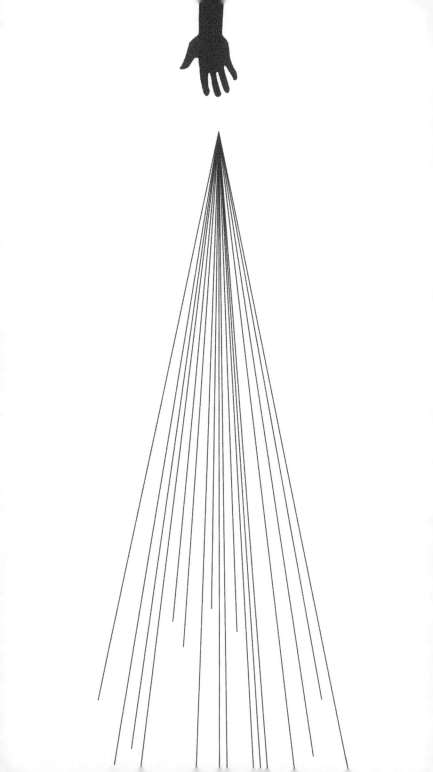

CONTENTS

IMPROVISE, GIRL, IMPROVISE

LILITH LATINI

DOLL

He instructs me to untie his shoelaces
with my teeth and addresses me as Doll.
Not dismissive, but tender and reverential.
Doll. He asked for permission first.

His forefinger is under my chin as I slide my hands
   down
his body. Our eyes do not look away from each
   other,
he beholds me like a prize. I can't understand it.
My heels meet my ass and I move onto my knees.

After we first slept together he watched me
pull my stockings back on, said he should
be paying to watch. Then he asked if he could call
   me Doll.

I didn't trust him. It was the beginning of my
   transition.
He waited for me to walk across a room with
   hungry patience.
I still remind myself to see others' sincerity.

Back then, I cast my eyes down and hurried for
   clothes.
It hurt, like a joke. He dangled what it felt like
to be cared for at me, and I refused to be fooled.

GLORIA SPEAKS

Listen Patti, before I became
your muse, I was my own, steadily
stitching a disparate body together,
telling the story of how

the Pine Barrens only grow by
lighting fire to their lost limbs.
We're both Jersey girls. You know each pine
cone's tiered shell embodies flame,
ready to reach and open upon ignition.
Red needles over the sandy soil –
torch the damn thing so it grows.

I retold myself this story at
the precipice of choosing.

I walked up those stairs, to your room and
the couch where I laid your mouth and
that jagged howl: "I just made her mine!"

As though you groan of your own accord,
as if the sight of me doesn't possess you.
Don't you think I've cast this spell before?
Go ahead, babe. Keep singing.

SWILL

i.

Harlequin lips quiver and I scrape
my shoes on the steps. After last call
my best thoughts come crawling:

I will plant a garden, read a book a week, convince
a white person *Who Framed Roger Rabbit?* is racist.

My hands grasp on one metal fence post.
The next. Concentrate. Hip swing left,
then right, one heel stuck between
two paving stones. Stand still.

ii.

Morning glares, and I hunch into my purse.
Mascara, perfume, receipts. Where
are my sunglasses? Oxblood sunspots scribble
the street, bright heat under my skin. Look up.

iii.

Throw back my shoulders and pull at
my skirt. Tongue tastes like ash.
Clear the phlegm from my throat.

Decide: today,
at least for a few hours,
I will not dribble down some dirty sink's drain.

Just breathe.
It's a long block
to the train. Walk.

CONFIRMATION

When I told the therapist my friends forced me to play as the Wonder Woman action figure, I was eight and cognizant of the lie. My scarred hand on the scalding stove. At thirteen we took on saint's names in Confirmation and became adults of the church. False words won't make it to God's ears. I was like: these shoes are so ugly, another masculine name sounds great, thanks, whatever, amen.

VISITING FAMILY

When I walked up my family's driveway, a bird circled
overhead looking for the dead thing it smelled.
All year I loosed stitches from my lips with violet nails.

The ash grey dress may have been much, my parents
not expecting make-up. I fiddled with the hem
of my skirt over unshaven legs, eyes darting
while words fell from my mouth like rain.
Mom and Dad paled at my unmovable certainty.

They believed I charged like a train, bright light
and steam that broke against their turned heads,
but I'm not sudden or new. I've only been walking.
I told them noon. They should have been expecting me.

GINA, TRINA, AND ESMERALDA
the creation of a tranny tough as acrylic nails

i.

Esmeralda meditated on false eyelashes
right before the drug store closed. Purple feathers
or gold rhinestones? He floated to the counter,
both in hand, and purred to the cashier,

"Do you get a discount, darling?"
"Um. No."
"Oh. I was almost jealous of your entire life!"
Money changed hands and the doors flung open.

ii.

The phone propped next to the shower.
Gina screamed at it,
"I told you I had plans!"
Water off, curtain open, unfurled steam.

"Maybe I'll run into you, baby."
His body sliced the heat.
Gina rubbed the mirror, practiced his pout.
"It's going to be a long night.
We'll be on fire. You may see me
come morning. If we're lucky. "

iii.

Trina slept under sixteen blankets:
down comforters, crocheted yarn,
fleece. The pile rose and fell
with his long breaths.

Unworn high heels along the walls:
clear plastic, patent leather, peep toed.
Glitter spilled on his bathroom sink
next to the wrench and scrawlings
in a notebook titled *Can I Become?*

iv.

Gina drove and Esmeralda blew on his still-wet
   nails.
One more night until the moon was full, but Gina
   cried,
"It's tonight! I don't care what your astrologer says.
Darling, that round thing is rolling all through me."

He shivered and giggled. Esmeralda licked his lips.
Esmeralda held out his hand and asked,
"Are we ready to push this chick out of the nest?"
Gina twined his fingers with Esmeralda's. Each
agreed to the night's work.

They parked at Trina's house, threw the door open.
Sang, "Wake up sweetness, the night's ripening!
We've got things to do and places to see!"

v.

Three creatures in front of a mirror.
"Can you glue these on for me?"
"Oh, I love that. So pearly,
bioluminescent." "Move over!"
"Bitch, keep your skirt on!
I do not live to please you!"
"Does my butt look right in this?"
"Yes. Yes! Can I borrow that?"
"Wait. Do these sequins catch
too much light?" "Never enough light."
"Will you zip up my dress?"
"Of course, darling."

He kisses Trina's cheek, fingertips on his shoulders.

vi.

Bodies like blades breezed down the sidewalk,
through the bar's door. They slouch off jackets
and drop their purses. Gina and Esmeralda stalked
to the bar and ordered Trina a drink. That one sat on
    a stool,
studying his face in a compact. The bartender
    winked, their
glossed ruby lips, black glittering eyes, rhinestone
    and feather
lashes embossed in the dim light. This paint was for
    battle,
to claim a territory, a space. Steel mace shoulders swung,
legs whipped, hips fired shotgun bullets.

vii.

Gina batted his eyes at shirtless men: pale, blonde,
   blurred.
Knife legs minced around the throbbing bodies,
he blew a kiss, pouted. Trina downed a second
   whiskey.

Polo shirts, bronzed chests, trucker caps and
Esmeralda hauling thirsty Trina into the crowd.
He flung that sequined body like a pickaxe between
the dancers. Trina's pearl teeth glinted as she
   turned.

viii.

Gina, Trina, and Esmeralda dug through her skin,
ripped the lid off a boarded up well behind that
   stomach.
She guzzled the liquid, starved for a self bound by
   rotten
wood and rusted nails. Between bark and howl,
   bark and howl,

 Gina shrieked at Trina, "I knew it, I knew! Don't
   stop working!"
Trina shrieked, drunk, feet on fire; milky eyed boys
   escaped to dance
in the corner. Esmeralda sang, "Water the seeds
   with honey, bunny,
Water those dried out seeds!"

ix.

The next morning Gina and Esmeralda stood over
  Trina's
briny body in bed covered partly by a sheet, lipstick
  smeared
and rhinestones stuck to the pillow. "Should we
  take her
for breakfast?" Esmeralda asked. "Oh no." Gina
  smiled.
"What this girl needs is to take a walk." He took
  Esmeralda's hand,
and they flounced away in the early afternoon light,
  satisfied.

JUDY GARLAND AND THE STONEWALL GIRLS

A video of Judy howling *Down
With Love*, the microphone cord
thrown over her shoulder, shaky finger
barbed and pointed at her audience.

Some blamed the Stonewall Riots on her death.
Cue a montage of queens' tears fallen
on radios playing *Somewhere Over the Rainbow*,
panty hose hung on radiators, dresses flung on the
    floor,
doors open to let the June heat smear through.

I will not rise on the stage like Judy, some white
lightning rod, lilting with gestures barely hinged
to my body and bathe in that limelight this year.

Hair unfurled, the Stonewall Girls
now lay caged or murdered. Don't send me
out of the closet and into the streets alone.
Someone has to help me out of my strappy shoes
    before we run.

I won't wear a radiant smile, wait for the script,
a calm white trans woman standing by
as cis white people process in formal wear.
Under those hot lights tears dry quickly,
but I won't cry under those lights alone.

Down with love, Judy said, the root of all
midnight blues. Down with love, the flowers
and rice and shoes. Down with eyes, romantic and
   stupid.

Don't send me out alone and undone,
an ivory decoy full of rice and rose petals,
as though these streets are not a battleground.

INCISIONS

Some might believe in the elegance
of unfolding butterfly wings,
covered in change's pearly tears
and backlit by a summer sunrise.

Instead: stern mumbling professionals
in green scrubs who place scalpels
against skin; the weak terror of knowing
I will wake in visceral pain,
immobile, and changed.

Blood soaked layers
of a cocoon peeled away, yes,
gauze ribboning out from between
my legs like some bondage, like a skin,
maybe a snake's skin. No – my skin,
and what I shed.

I sought this.
Sorry, not sorry.

I hope healing greets me like some flame-maned
thing who guns her motorcycle's engine and peels
    off
with me straddled behind her, like a bullet so hot
she finally fuses me into a single piece.

THRESHOLDS

I am winded. As though the slog toward the threshold was enough, the prize to now watch the past slough off. I hoped a chariot would be waiting, commanded by a muscle-bound chauffeur who would compliment me on my grace. We would be propelled into the future by the force of his admiration for my spunkiness and incredible hair. But I know the future only breaks open at the insistence of choking, hacking with turbulent focus at the gilded door to feminine success.

SNOWED IN

Two half-read books are pushed
to the edge of the bed,
and he puts a pillow
under my pelvis
so my ass is arched at
just the angle he wants.

Things a boy I once fucked told me:
just a cobbled body, low groan,
relentlessly slim hips.
Then he pushes inside me.

My mind tries again to recoil
from the reality of touch, but

his hand grabs a fistful of my hair and
the other grips my hip.
I buck towards his mouth.
He bites the freckles on my skin.

My attention unfolds to the ends of my limbs

LOVEDOG VS PIRANHACLAW
confrontations with melancholy

i.

Piranhaclaw layers one arm over
the other; silver tipped fingers
draw circles on the glossy
table next to each elbow.

She says she wants to play a game.

Lovedog leans back in her seat.
She knows opposition
only announces itself when

the game is afoot.
She gulps and her heart slips
through the sinkhole in her chest.

ii.

After Piranhaclaw leaves, Lovedog looks in
her clutch and finds missing her tools
for survival: billy club, cyanide pill
and the keys to her jet.

She looks up in time to see them leap
toward the horizon: Piranhaclaw, her
engine, propellors, and riveted hull.

iii.

Lovedog goes to the basement to assess her
    resources.
Even without the preferred methods, one must
    survive.
Melancholy rotted her foundation.
Piranhaclaw may outwit her.
Lovedog presses her paws to her eyes and thinks,
Improvise, girl, improvise!

iv.

Piranhaclaw touches down on the grayest beach.
Sand rises from a stagnant shore
to meet splintered, flaking trees.

She steps on a twig that snaps. One crack
sprung from a gnarled, withered limb left lying
so long it won't soften in humidity or rain.

Cloud-filtered daylight over the crooked things.

v.

Lovedog stands at the edge of a sparse, moist place.

Stolid trees wilt in the humidity.
There's an impasse ahead, she can feel it,
and hopes that she brought enough dynamite.

Never caught with the right tools,
never at the right time, always at
that place where land begins its slow
dissolution at ocean's touch.

She hops from one haunch
to the other and says aloud,
Gut check?

and tears a bitebrawling howl from her chest.

vi.

Lovedog is on the scent,
even with offshore winds whipping at the coast.

Smell: the strongest sense tied to memory, or:
how to detect the nearness of that which would
   destroy you before it might find you.

vii.

Surface is cold.
Hard, smooth, cold.

She pulls at her tethered paws.
Tight, hard, smooth, cold.

Smells like wood, dead wood,
dead so long it hardly smells.

Could open her eyes, but would rather
whimper, whimper, whimper.

Lovedog feels breath against her shoulder.

vii.

The shrill questions of woe:
Do you know how I caught you?
Why I brought you here?

With the thumb and forefinger of each hand
she tears open the lids of Lovedog's eyes.

Rivulets of blood spring from the tips of
Piranhaclaw's nails
and run into Lovedog's sight.

With a sniff, Piranhaclaw says,
You smell of meat and inexperience.

IN HEAT

It's the movie theater air conditioning,
his hand clutching the back of her neck,
her obvious rapture.

Pierce Brosnan paws at Terri Hatcher —
my seven year old skin chills.

Picture me buried under horse print blankets,
boiling with fantasies of how a woman
possesses a man:

I crawl out of the surf, wet,
chain mail bikini against raw
salted skin. Cut to an unattended
cigarette on the nightstand. Smoke curls
over me, arranged
like a Bond Girl on the bed,
moaning, "Oh, James..."

He never said anything back.
After all, he was only a pillow.

Some nights, I dreamt of a woman
who possesses herself:

I crawl out of the surf, wet,
chain mail bikini against
raw salted skin. I stand.
I don't squint in the sunlight.

WELLNESS

Someone told me a religion states that in
the last millennium or so of humanity's
existence people will defy the gender
binary. Though not in such terms,
more that men will become women and
vice versa - apocalyptic.
Another said Fallon Fox transitioned
to legally beat other women, to
fulfill a misogynist impulse. Though not
in such terms, more that she was a crazy
dude hellbent on beating chicks.

That night I dreamt of a card spread that spelled
deadbolts on house doors and a lit blowtorch.
End Times brought me a new lipstick,
the note read, "Can you hear them whispering?"

Fists swinging, iron hot. If I am an unthing
or one made to bring the end, at least I know
how to solder the rubble together, unlike you.

BY NIGHT'S END

The sun crossed his blank neck,
silent motion of a chewing jaw.

Outside Bergdorf Goodman we ate
greased sandwiches before work,
filled in a dialogue for the mannequins.

"Did you ever think I could be so beautiful,
    husband?"
"Why, I never knew one might have
a more beautiful bloom after their first."

And he sighed, then sighed, shifted
his shoulders left, crossed his legs right.

He asked me to write something
about block parties and breezes when he lay
in the wide open window. I winced.
His easy tenderness couldn't revive
our wilting relation.

My heart hung
like a mannequin in a frigid pose.
I crafted an immovable distance
between myself and sweetness.

I did not explain, or whisper goodbye. I wrote:
Bluegreen lanterns swing slowly over
crowded streets, groan of diverted traffic,
grinding cargo ships whisper against bubbled sea.

TEENAGE DREAM

"I'm gonna get your heart racing in my skintight jeans,
be your teenage dream tonight" — Katy Perry

The bus bumps along the road,
and he offers his headphones
to let me listen to his favorite song.

> "Step barefoot on a cliff's edge,
> then the rough to nothing crumble
> under calloused heels –
> a body paused,
> then plummeting."

At night, in shadows, he touched me,
and at night, tossing over in my bed
I turned on a lamp. There was a pen
on the nightstand. With each swirling
letter I coiled our whispers and kisses
onto the page, under the light.

> "A python's tongue flicks
> just before she flexes that grip
> woven with adrenaline and want."

When he betrayed me and resolved to date a girl
I turned on the lamp and the overhead light and
the ceiling fan to clear the shadows, the dream, and
  the humidity.

"At the bottom, which is the peak:
lips spit an orange seed into my lined palm,
other hand rolls a cherry tomato over
fingers. The burst, each thing
grows and twists, burrows into skin.
Thick bark and flat bristled leaves,
roots sore and swollen fill each lung."

FITZY BUTCH, DUDETTE LAMONGE, AND DONNA PECAN

i.

We spent the mornings crushing sequins,
  dusted the glitter over eggs. We ate.

ii.

Fitzy Butch wakes – dirty denim,
coffee, daffodils trimmed in their vase
that splits light in the window. By noon,
rabbit skins stretched on the porch

iii.

Dudette LaMonge wakes – the cat crawls
over gold lamé, champagne, a lightning bolt
lamp splits light in the window. By noon,
scallop-lace panties hung on the line.

iv.

Donna Pecan wakes – cracked teacup,
dusty iris petals over the sill, a crystal
ashtray splits light in the window. By noon,
oil slicked skillet soaks in the sink

v.

Leather vest, silk blazer, fedora.
Sheer rhinestone-studded cape, booty shorts.
Strapless jumpsuit, nude pumps, hoops.

In the foyer we hold each other's wrists.
Every morning, after gnawing for nutrition and
before entering the world's harsh light

we address that thin skin which
bubbles with blood.
No prayers, no spells. Three witnesses.

vi.

Rack after sale rack, and but one
half-worthy tube of stolen lipstick.

The three of them recline
drinking regrettable mall coffee,
more chocolate syrup on ice than anything.

There's the general crowd's glued eyes –
then two parents with two gawping children
sidle up and say, "Wow, those outfits –"

It's all wings, shrill screams
and comets from the sky.

Fitzy: "Who raised you to stare at strangers like
    that?"
Dudette: "Some people have no manners."
Donna: "Go leer at something in need of your
    validation, please."

Sequins, a precursor to scales – as in
lips, a warning of teeth. They bite.

vii.

Fitzy, how do I look?
Dudette, how do I look?
Donna, how do I look?

Caged animal now walking,
Poison-slicked frog lounging on a leaf.

viii.

Each day we lift the anchor.

Six arms at the barnacled chain.
Thirty fingers tangle in the links.

As if to begin meant a simple shedding,

all the tethers snapped off like
some cheap panties. No.

Six arms, thirty fingers,
ninety-sixish gritted teeth.

SO MANY WAYS TO SNAP OUT OF IT

I've washed my dream catcher
in lavender and sage to no effect –
it's too much, too sticky, like chewing
taffy dropped in the ocean's surf.
The camera's rolling – Look sad
and unstoppably determined!
A little more! Pageant!

Open mouth oh as in ocean,
the waves conducted at lunar whim,
swollen, shallow, ragged rush.

I'm naked, but someone yells, keep going!
So I'm at it again, peeling off my hair,
follicle by follicle, then my toes,
flicking off each nail.
Snap skin up from musculature
like an old front hall rug and
it's all nerve endings out. Pose.
Nobody says anything.
The air and I hang still, aching.

VISITING THE PHILADELPHIA ART MUSEUM ONLY TO FIND OUT *NUDE DESCENDING A STAIRCASE* IS IN PARIS

Sometimes I dream
about angular structures
and smudged colors tumbling
down a frame.

Sometimes when I love my body
I see it as a picture:
harsh beauty
in purposeful motion,
dark shadow and cream expanses

hung upon a tentative wish
to step out towards
a hungry viewer.

Today I am hungry, wandering through
the galleries past Picasso, Renoir, and
an unexpected, unfinished Klimt.

A woman rises with an ambiguously
exultant face and a blank body
overcome by flowers, the blooms
like iced cupcakes.

"The young woman, a beautiful Viennese,
successfully courted suicide after a lover left her.
Does Klimt posit suicide's glory, here,
in this woman's expression?"

Once, after another man said, how could I ever?
I lay in bed wearing my best lingerie, drank
    champagne,
thought about my desolate body and love.

Yes, I've desired a constriction
of my experience, for the gift of my throat cut open.
Why bother to live any kind of life?

It is not beautiful or romantic to dream of holding
a gun's barrel against my chest, throat, head.
I get so sick of needing to make a point.

Suddenly, there's Cy Twombly and
Shades of Eternal Night.

Keep moving.
It won't always be night,
even in the myths where

"a fog rises in success off the bloodied
Trojans absent from the canvas."

I refuse to hold the image
in my heart, could never let
my blues turn indigo to navy,
slate to charcoal to onyx.
Of course, they have.

Finally, Duchamp and a notice
that the painting I dream about is on tour in Paris.

There are other placards noting how
"the artist divests from the sensory
in favor of intellect."

I wonder. The nude, the staircase, the witness,
that visual moment of intimacy;

It's an intellectual experience if you work for it,
    maybe,
if you are rejecting the intimacy, if you are
    theorizing the body.

In the tentative dream that I hold in my heart,
he does not ask how could he ever.
He says that I smell good and
asks if I will let him hold me.

FACT OF A FLAT

Tire's rim against rubber against
pavement. Car hunched over
its warped wheel, and nothing
to do but haul the thing up
on a jack. She hasn't traveled
far enough, she hasn't traveled
this far to stumble.

Separate nuts from bolts. After
the last rusted seal cracks, shuck
the wasted wheel from its joint –
trade for the spare's uneven twist –
Get out while the chance is there.

CABBAGE SOUP

Corn husks rot beneath autumn's
cabbage. Small, neat purple bruises
in long lines. Their wrinkled frames
fan open. Harvest moon full and empty,
its orange glare obscures the stars. Already
brown October leaves flake across
the field. Night's crystal frost on the full-bloomed
food. All of us out in the field, living
a tulle-draped fantasy, gathering cabbages
and ourselves together. Cackle and call
our bruises food, sustaining our resilience.
We'll eat those fetid bruises, boil them
in soup. Save the faded broth,
let each limp piece float to the surface.

EMBODIED DESIRE

The gulf between house and home, body and embodied is full of drowning, deep breaths that flood lungs with desiccated fish, flakes from hulls of sunken ships. Wait. Another man fumbling with her long pencil skirt's zipper. Contemplate the record of struggling with that useless vessel, organizing the tonnage, twisting each rivet tight, adjusting sails that fail even to catch a breeze, unable to navigate toward any direction until nerve-endings with their flint-tipped fingers come sparking, relentless,

HELLOOOOOOO? FEEL THAT? JUST LIKE THAT? FEEL YOUR CLIT IN THIS LIGHTNING LIPPED CREATURE'S GROWLING MOUTH? FEEL THAT TONGUE, THAT TONGUE THRUMMING, HIS BREATH CONDENSING ON YOUR SKIN, AND HIS TONGUE LICKING UP EACH DROP?

Belly up like a beached mermaid, cool air puckering skin, his hands reaching to pinch her nipples, she realizes she's panting and says "don't you dare stop, daddy."

WOLVES

Behind the serrated leaves hide
a blackberry cane's heaviest
globules of fruit.

Behind that dense cluster
of laden canes are
his fingers, my grip,
his pulse, my thighs.

Muzzles off, pants around
our ankles and the briefest
moment of sincerity amidst
the distending dusk.

I didn't need him to stay.
The quick night takes me
when he leaves, the cool
night takes my hand.

All the darlings beyond the shadowed
tree line, gnashing their teeth. We run.

TAKE A BATH!

Light a candle, you filthy thing.
Shut the door and put on that torch song you love.
Let the tub's water scald and stretch your skin.
How long since you last scrubbed behind your ears?
Shut your yammering yap and listen to your
heartbeat.
   pulse: pulse:
         pulse: pulse:

ABOUT THE AUTHOR

Lilith Latini is a poet and party girl based in Philadelphia, PA. Her work has appeared in *Troubling The Line, XOJane, Trans Poets Will Burn Your House Down*, and her 2013 zine *Lip Print*. She is a graduate of the University of North Carolina at Asheville. *Improvise, Girl, Improvise* is her first book.

ACKNOWLEDGEMENTS

I would most like to thank Cat Fitzpatrick, who was extremely patient in helping develop and polish this body of work. Athena Thiessen, Charles Theonia, and Benjamin Crabstick for critically reading this in altered forms. Holly Iglesias, Melissa Plotts, and Caroline Wilson who all have aided and abetted my poetic practice so far. Mattilda Bernstein Sycamore for the text "So Many Ways to Sleep Badly" that inspired the poem "So Many Ways to Snap Out of It."

ABOUT HELIOTROPE

Heliotrope is a dedicated series of poetry books by transgender authors. We value writing which is clear, direct, beautiful and complex. The poetry we publish is a challenge. It's a tool, but it's also a dare to use that tool: to talk more; to think harder; to believe in yourself *and* question yourself; maybe even to write some poems of your own.

In 2015, Heliotrope will publish books by Lilith Latini, Charles Theonia, Tyler Vile and Kay Ulanday Barrett.

Heliotrope is an imprint of Topside Press and is edited by Cat Fitzpatrick. Cat teaches literature at Rutgers University - Newark and organizes the Trans Poets Workshop NYC.

Poets are welcome to join the Trans Poets Workshop. More information is available at transpoets.com.

Submissions of poetry manuscripts are welcome year-round at topsidepress.com.

20101145R00033

Made in the USA
Middletown, DE
15 May 2015